Pebble®
Plus

(EXPLORE)
LIFE CYCLES

A Bean's
Life Cycle

by Mary R. Dunn

CAPSTONE PRESS
a capstone imprint

Pebble Plus is published by Capstone Press,
1710 Roe Crest Drive, North Mankato, Minnesota 56003
www.mycapstone.com

Library of Congress Cataloging-in-Publication Data
Library of Congress Cataloging-in-Publication data is available on the Library of Congress website.
ISBN 978-1-5157-7051-0 (library binding)
ISBN 978-1-5157-7057-2 (paperback)
ISBN 978-1-5157-7063-3 (eBook PDF)

Editorial Credits
Anna Butzer, editor; Kyle Grenz, designer
Wanda Winch, media researcher; Kathy McColley, production specialist

Photo Credits
Dreamstime: Onefivenine, 15; Shutterstock: Antonio Gravante, 17, Blaine Image, 19, Bogdan Wankowicz, 7, Denis Kovalenko, 2, 18, 20, FLariviere, 21, Jens Holzmann, cover, Katerina Veyevnik, 6, 14, Nikilev, 13, Peter Zijlstra, 1, Richard Griffin, 5, showcake, 9, View Factor Images, back cover, Voodoo Dot, 10, 24, YOROZU, 11

Note to Parents and Teachers

The Explore Life Cycles set supports national science standards related to life science. This book describes and illustrates the life cycle of beans. The images support early readers in understanding the text. The repetition of words and phrases helps early readers learn new words. This book also introduces early readers to subject-specific vocabulary words, which are defined in the Glossary section. Early readers may need assistance to read some words and to use the Table of Contents, Glossary, Read More, Internet Sites, Critical Thinking Questions, and Index sections of the book.

Printed and bound in China.
010408F17

Table of Contents

Planting Seeds

It is spring! Broad bean seeds are planted in soil. With water and warm temperatures, the bean seeds begin to change.

Tiny white roots break out of the seed
and reach down into the soil.
Roots bring nutrients
from the soil to the seed.
The roots hold the plant in place.

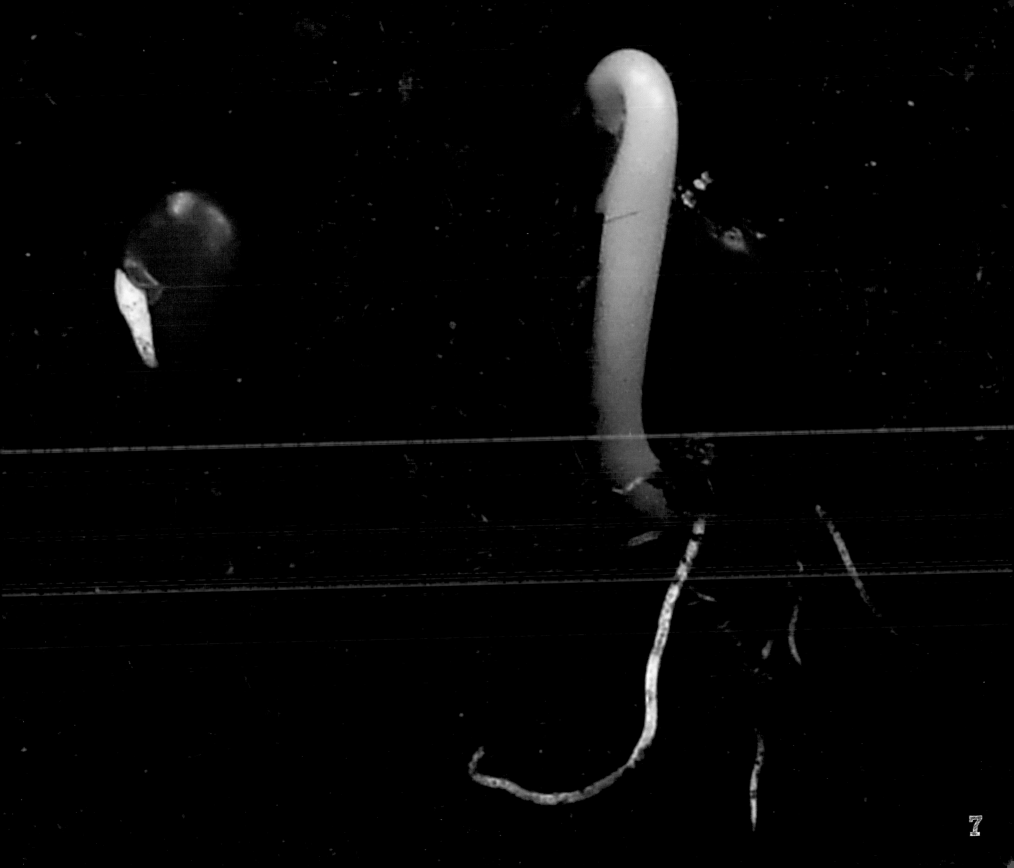

7

Sprouting Seeds

Soon, a bean shoot sprouts. It pops
through the soil and becomes the stem.
Tiny leaves on the stem start to grow.
The leaves begin to open.

Roots take in water from the soil.

The stems carry water to the leaves.

Leaves use water, air, and sunlight

to make food for the plant.

11

Flowering Plants

Flower buds appear at the bottom of the leaves. These black and white flowers have pollen. They also have a sweet juice called nectar.

13

Buzz! A bee lands on a flower to sip nectar. The bee has pollen on it from a different flower. The pollen will make beans grow.

Hanging Pods

Bean pods grow and the

flowers begin to die.

The pods are lumpy and thick.

They protect the seeds inside.

17

Bean plants have about 12 bean pods.

Each pod will have three to eight seeds.

Some pods are picked to eat.

Other pods dry out and pop open.

Their seeds fall out. These seeds

may become new plants in spring.

GLOSSARY

bud—a small shoot on a plant that grows into a leaf or a flower

nectar—a sweet liquid found in many flowers

pod—a long case that holds the seeds of certain plants, such as peas

pollen—a powder made by flowers to help them create new seeds

root—the part of the plant that is underground

shoot—the white stem growing out of a seed that becomes a plant

soil—top layer of ground where plants grow

stem—the part of a plant that connects the roots to the leaves

READ MORE

Colby, Jennifer. *Growing New Plants.* Ann Arbor, MI: Cherry Lake Publishing, 2014.

Rattini, Kristin Baird. *Seed to Plant.* National Geographic Readers. Washington D.C.: National Geographic Society, 2014.

Thomas, Patricia. *Green Bean! Green Bean*! Nevada City, CA: Dawn Publications, 2016.

INTERNET SITES

FactHound offers a safe, fun way to find Internet sites related to this book. All of the sites on FactHound have been researched by our staff.

Here's all you do:

Visit *www.facthound.com*

Type in this code: 9781515770510

Check out projects, games and lots more at **www.capstonekids.com**

CRITICAL THINKING QUESTIONS

1. Reread the text on page 10. What important thing do stems do for plants?

2. How do bees help bean plants grow?

3. Find the word in the glossary that tells what part of the plant holds the bean seeds.

INDEX